Challenge FACTORY®

Challenge Factory Inc.
1235 Bay Street
Suite 700
Toronto, ON M5R 3K4
Canada

1-416-217-0777
www.ChallengeFactory.ca
ClientSupport@ChallengeFactory.ca

ISBN
Paperback: 978-1-7772284-4-6
PDF: 978-1-7772284-5-3
Authors: Lisa Taylor and Taryn Blanchard

Canada ⬥ **EMPLOYMENT ONTARIO** Ontario 🏵

Acknowledgments

Financial support for the second edition of *The Canadian Guide to Hiring Veterans* was generously provided by the Government of Ontario's Skills Development Fund as part of the Veteran Friendly Ontario (VFO) project.

We are grateful to the more than 100 employers—including small businesses, large enterprises, nonprofits, and others—that have participated in the Challenge Factory research, consulting, and training programs that informed this *Guide*. Working together, we have raised awareness about the benefits of hiring Veterans, provided employers with tools that make hiring easier, and drawn on Veterans' knowledge to make sure we get it right. See the research methodology to learn more about the participants involved in this important work.

Land acknowledgment

Challenge Factory acknowledges that our head office in Toronto is situated on the traditional lands of the Huron-Wendat, Petun, Haundenosaunee, Anishinaabe, and Mississauga Anishinaabe of New Credit. To learn more about the lands you live and work on, visit www.Native-Land.ca and www.Whose.Land.

TABLE OF CONTENTS

INTRODUCTION | THE HIDDEN TALENT ADVANTAGE: WHY HIRING VETERANS HELPS EMPLOYERS 1

Why create a Veteran hiring guide?. 2

Features of *The Canadian Guide to Hiring Veterans* 4

Become a certified Veteran Ready Employer. 5

PART 1 | TOOLS FOR HIRING AND RETAINING VETERANS 6

The complete Take Action checklist. 8

Will Veteran talent be successful in your organization?. 10

Understand your Veteran Quotient (VQ) 11

Military to civilian translation 14

Customize your recruitment materials. 18

How to find Veteran jobseekers. 25

Interviewing Veterans for a job 27

Onboarding new Veteran hires 31

PART 2 | HIRING SCENARIOS THAT BUST MYTHS ABOUT VETERANS 38

Hiring scenario 1 – The health myth 40

Hiring scenario 2 – The education myth 42

Hiring scenario 3 – The drill sergeant myth 44

Hiring scenario 4 – The failure-to-adapt myth. 46

Hiring scenario 5 – The civilian work awareness myth 48

Hiring scenario 6 – The easy-to-identify myth 50

Hiring scenario 7 – The cookie cutter myth 52

Hiring scenario 8 – The military skills myth 54

Hiring scenario 9 – The military culture myth. 56

**PART 3 | DATA-INFORMED HIRING APPROACHES:
MEASURING THE HIDDEN TALENT ADVANTAGE** **58**

Do Veteran hiring resources really help employers?. 59

How Veterans act in the workplace 62

What you should know about the Veteran working profile 64

PART 4 | RESOURCES. **67**

RESEARCH METHODOLOGY. **70**

NOTES AND REFERENCES **76**

INTRODUCTION | THE HIDDEN TALENT ADVANTAGE: WHY HIRING VETERANS HELPS EMPLOYERS

Welcome employers, hiring managers, and everyone interested in hiring and retaining great talent. You've come to the right place. Whether you're here on behalf of a small business, nonprofit, or other organization, *The Canadian Guide to Hiring Veterans* will be a useful resource.

The world of work is changing, and so are industries and communities. In the past, many organizations were able to focus narrowly on their core business or mandate. Today, however, labour market fluctuations, legislation changes, shifts in worker behaviours and attitudes, diversity, equity, and inclusion (DEI) imperatives, and an increase in demand for mental wellness supports at work mean every organization has to prioritize its people in new ways. This creates new challenges and opportunities for employers.

At the heart of Canada's labour market is the worker: the real human who shapes and is shaped by their workplace. No organization can succeed without the right people, and building a workforce—big or small—takes effort, tenacity, and oftentimes course correction. Amidst tough labour market forces, the leader's job has become more complex, and employers must contend with a host of questions:

- Where are all the qualified jobseekers hiding?

- What happens when we struggle to build a strong workforce?

- What happens when succession planning pipelines are weak for our next-generation senior leadership roles?

- How can we find the right staff, hire them, and keep them in a time when churn seems to be the norm?

This easy-to-use Challenge Factory resource offers a simple but powerful solution: **Become a Veteran Friendly Employer.**

Becoming a Veteran Friendly Employer is proven to help you recruit the right people to your organization and keep them long-term. Learning hiring skills and human resources (HR) approaches that focus on one specific hidden talent pool—Canada's military Veterans—will also improve your overall hiring, HR processes, work culture, and career management. Both Veterans and other jobseekers want to work for Veteran Friendly Employers, making this approach to hiring a critical advantage for employers.

Why create a Veteran hiring guide?

Military Veterans are one of Canada's most adaptable, versatile, and hidden talent pools. This is a vital opportunity that can help employers of all stripes meet their organizational needs in today's challenging and changing world of work.

The Canadian Guide to Hiring Veterans is designed to:

1. Help organizations that have limited HR resources and recruitment capacity improve their hiring process and employee retention programs.

2. Destigmatize Veterans in and outside the workplace, and clarify exactly why they make such a valuable talent pool and recruitment source.

The second edition of the *Guide* has been updated to reflect current labour market and hiring conditions. It also includes enhanced tools and analysis based on what has been learned since the publication of the first edition. Finally, the ecosystem that supports Veterans transitioning from the military into civilian life has become more organized and easier to navigate for employers. As a result, we've streamlined the resources we offer, especially in Part 4, into fewer and more effective access points.

> The successful participation of Veterans in Canada's civilian workforce is important not only for them and their families, but also for the country's employers and labour markets as a whole. Challenge Factory's business and workplace have both benefitted immensely from working with Veterans, either as employees or clients. We hope this *Guide* helps you reap the same benefits.
>
> **– Taryn Blanchard, Lisa Taylor, and the Challenge Factory team**

What should you know?

- Small organizations in Canada are facing precarious and unusual labour market and hiring conditions—and need to find the *right* employees to hire. Veterans make quality employees who can fill labour and skills shortages, step into leadership roles, and contribute to overall organizational success.

- Misperceptions, stereotypes, and biases about Veterans are common. Some are perpetuated by popular culture, while others are more subtle and implicit. These myths create real barriers for Veterans trying to find work and prevent employers from viewing them as a viable recruitment source.

- Stereotypes are not useful. Every Veteran is different and should be assessed for employability on their own merits.

- Veterans bring a diverse set of experiences, perspectives, and ideas to their workplaces. Challenge Factory's research proves they have a unique "working profile" that can make them excellent employees.

- Many employers and hiring managers have a low Veteran Quotient (VQ). This means they can make incorrect assumptions about Veterans in the workplace. An important way for employers to improve their VQ score is to gain more direct exposure to Veterans and military communities.

- Becoming a Veteran Friendly Employer doesn't only help employers hire and retain Veterans. It also makes their overall hiring and HR practices better and easier. Creating a strong Employment Value Proposition plays an important role in the development of an employer's hiring skills and work culture.

Features of *The Canadian Guide to Hiring Veterans*

Practical, reusable hiring tools that will make recruitment, hiring, and onboarding easier. For all the employers and hiring managers struggling to find the right employees, this *Guide* will offer a real and adaptable action plan.

Busting myths about Veterans in the workplace, through the use of relatable hiring scenarios, so it's clear why these talented workers should be your next hire.

Evidence-based learning from Challenge Factory's research about the impact of using Veteran hiring resources and how Veterans really act in civilian workplaces.

Resources compiled in one convenient place to help you become a Veteran Friendly Employer.

Notable acronyms:

CAF – Canadian Armed Forces

EVP – Employment Value Proposition

VAC – Veterans Affairs Canada

Attention to our print readers

In the digital version of *The Canadian Guide to Hiring Veterans*, the green-coloured text is clickable, opening websites or jumping to other sections within the publication. For full access to this feature of the *Guide*, download your free digital copy at www.ChallengeFactory.ca/VeteranHiringGuide.

Become a certified Veteran Ready Employer

The Canadian Guide to Hiring Veterans will help you become a Veteran Friendly Employer. Want to elevate your capacity to attract and hire Veterans even more?

Complete Challenge Factory's free **MasterClass in Hiring: Tap into the Hidden Talent Pool of Canada's Veterans** to become a certified Veteran Ready Employer.

MasterClass features

- 5 learning modules that build on *The Canadian Guide to Hiring Veterans*
- Template for creating your own hiring Action Plan
- You get to choose your own learning path

What do you get when you complete the MasterClass?

1. Certificate of Completion
2. Veteran Ready badge and toolkit
3. Listing on Challenge Factory's website of Veteran Ready Employers

Join the growing list of Veteran Ready Employers across Canada.

Enroll in the MasterClass for free.

The hiring process is different for every employer. This means taking action to bring great military Veterans into your organization can also differ for every employer. Part 1 moves you through the process to become Veteran Friendly from beginning to end, offering steps, tips, and activities you can use in your hiring and retention journey. Approach them with an open mind and modify them to suit your own unique needs.

This *Guide* is designed to help you shift from being someone who has a general interest in hidden talent pools to being a Veteran Friendly Employer that Veterans and other job candidates seek out as a preferred workplace. Taking action will help you make that change, which in turn will make all future hiring cycles easier, more effective, and worthwhile investments.

Taking action: The Veteran hiring process

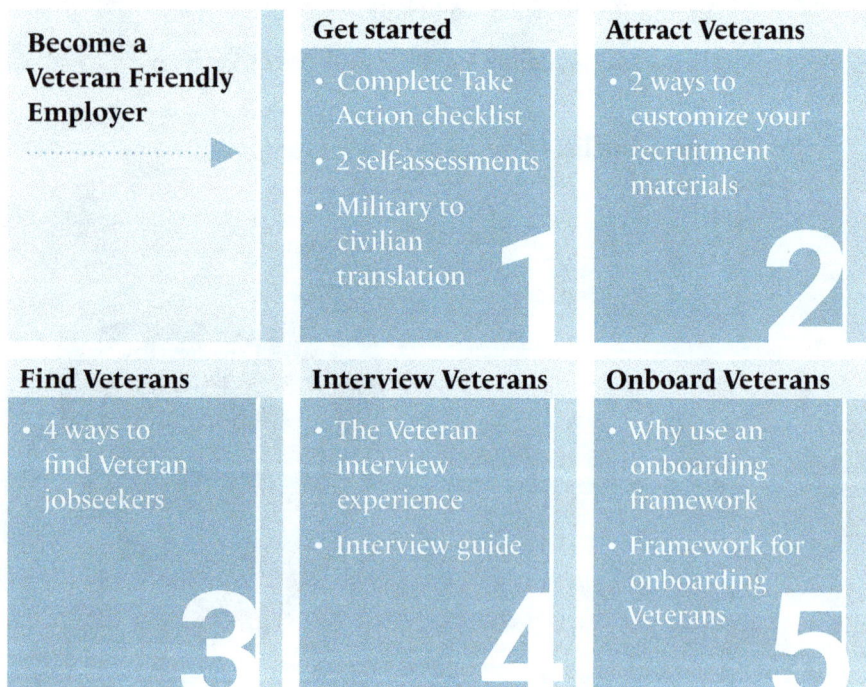

Become a Veteran Friendly Employer

Get started
- Complete Take Action checklist
- 2 self-assessments
- Military to civilian translation

1

Attract Veterans
- 2 ways to customize your recruitment materials

2

Find Veterans
- 4 ways to find Veteran jobseekers

3

Interview Veterans
- The Veteran interview experience
- Interview guide

4

Onboard Veterans
- Why use an onboarding framework
- Framework for onboarding Veterans

5

Learn from Lisa: Effective hiring is a skill

Lisa Taylor, Challenge Factory's Founder and President, is a small business owner with previous experience at large enterprises. When she managed large teams in these settings, she was often counseled to "hire slow and fire fast."

Rushing to hire a job candidate simply to get an opening filled and keeping an employee on who's clearly not a good fit both negatively affect an organization's productivity and culture. But sometimes "hire slow and fire fast" is much easier said than done—as Lisa discovered when she moved into the small business sector.

Small organizations of all types experience different pressures and constraints than large enterprises. Hiring often happens quickly and without robust processes. Lisa has found that when there's work that needs doing (which is always), her immediate priority can easily shift to bringing someone on board as fast as possible. Sometimes these quick hires turn into star employees. Other times, critical skills or suitability get overlooked. It's very tempting to fill the position as fast as possible and move on. Other business owners have expressed similar tendencies to her.

An important skill that Lisa had to develop is questioning the priority placed on speedy hiring (at the expense of proper candidate vetting), as well as the discomfort and resistance to letting someone go (even after doubts have arisen about their employment). Hiring can be an exhausting, time-consuming process—and learning how to do it effectively is part of every leader's professional development.

In today's labour market, even leaders within large enterprises feel pressure to act quicker to ensure candidates are not lost or team capacity remains high. Because job candidates now have more options and choices than previously imagined, what makes a job stand out is who the employee is working with and the environment they're working in. An organization's culture and team relationships are actually the best antidote to challenging labour market forces.

The complete Take Action checklist

This checklist synthesizes all the steps, tips, and activities presented in *The Canadian Guide to Hiring Veterans*. Use it to stay organized and on track during your Veteran hiring journey, from beginning to end.

Get started

Take the *Guide's* self-assessments ⸱⸱⸱⸱⸱⸱⸱⸱⸱⸱⸱⸱⸱⸱⸱⸱⸱⸱⸱⸱⸱⸱⸱⸱⸱⸱⸱⸱⸱⸱⸱⸱⸱⸱⸱⸱⸱⸱ ☐
   Will Veteran talent be successful in your organization? (page 10) ⸱⸱ ☐
   Understand your Veteran Quotient (page 11) ⸱⸱⸱⸱⸱⸱⸱⸱⸱⸱⸱⸱⸱⸱⸱⸱⸱⸱⸱⸱⸱⸱ ☐
Tackle confusing military language (page 14) ⸱⸱⸱⸱⸱⸱⸱⸱⸱⸱⸱⸱⸱⸱⸱⸱⸱⸱⸱⸱⸱⸱⸱⸱⸱ ☐

Attract Veterans

Customize your recruitment materials ⸱⸱⸱⸱⸱⸱⸱⸱⸱⸱⸱⸱⸱⸱⸱⸱⸱⸱⸱⸱⸱⸱⸱⸱⸱⸱⸱⸱⸱⸱⸱⸱ ☐
   Use Veteran Friendly job postings (page 18) ⸱⸱⸱⸱⸱⸱⸱⸱⸱⸱⸱⸱⸱⸱⸱⸱⸱⸱⸱⸱⸱ ☐
     Explain why Veteran jobseekers should consider
     your organization ⸱⸱⸱ ☐
     Describe your organization's Veteran hiring goals ⸱⸱⸱⸱⸱⸱⸱⸱⸱⸱ ☐
     Describe your organization's workforce diversity practices
     or policy ⸱⸱⸱ ☐
     Profile any Veterans already on staff ⸱⸱⸱⸱⸱⸱⸱⸱⸱⸱⸱⸱⸱⸱⸱⸱⸱⸱⸱⸱⸱⸱⸱⸱⸱ ☐
     Explore the websites of enterprises that have Veteran
     hiring programs ⸱⸱⸱ ☐
   Create a strong Employment Value Proposition (page 19) ⸱⸱⸱⸱⸱⸱ ☐

Find Veterans

Look for referrals (page 25) ⸱⸱⸱⸱⸱⸱⸱⸱⸱⸱⸱⸱⸱⸱⸱⸱⸱⸱⸱⸱⸱⸱⸱⸱⸱⸱⸱⸱⸱⸱⸱⸱⸱⸱⸱⸱⸱⸱ ☐
Join VAC's Veteran Employer mailing list ⸱⸱⸱⸱⸱⸱⸱⸱⸱⸱⸱⸱⸱⸱⸱⸱⸱⸱⸱⸱⸱⸱⸱⸱ ☐
Join the Hire a Veteran LinkedIn group ⸱⸱⸱⸱⸱⸱⸱⸱⸱⸱⸱⸱⸱⸱⸱⸱⸱⸱⸱⸱⸱⸱⸱⸱⸱ ☐
Use Job Bank to post jobs ⸱⸱⸱⸱⸱⸱⸱⸱⸱⸱⸱⸱⸱⸱⸱⸱⸱⸱⸱⸱⸱⸱⸱⸱⸱⸱⸱⸱⸱⸱⸱⸱⸱⸱⸱⸱⸱ ☐
Adjust your approach (embrace trial and error) ⸱⸱⸱⸱⸱⸱⸱⸱⸱⸱⸱⸱⸱⸱⸱⸱⸱⸱ ☐

Interview Veterans

Use an interview guide (page 29) ······································· ☐
  1. Don't let Veterans downplay their successes ··············· ☐
  2. Make sure Veterans discuss their military experience ······· ☐
  3. Find Veterans' business acumen beneath military-civilian
     language mismatches ··· ☐
  4. Focus on Veterans' interview preparation ·················· ☐
  5. Lay out the next steps clearly ······························ ☐

Onboard Veterans

Create a formal onboarding program (page 31) ················· ☐
  Use the *Guide's* framework for onboarding Veterans ········· ☐
Create structures and processes for retaining Veterans long-term ····· ☐
  Check out the activities in Challenge Factory's *Retain and
  Gain* playbooks ·· ☐

Will Veteran talent be successful in your organization?

As with any big life change, Veterans face a number of challenges when they leave the military. This includes the need to adapt to an unfamiliar civilian job market and workplace. Veterans have the talent, but sometimes they need an employer to help get them over the finish line and into meaningful, rewarding employment.

This self-assessment will help you get a sense of how quickly a Veteran will adapt to your organization. All new hires require organization-specific training. It's just a matter of making sure to orient to Veterans' unique needs so they can begin contributing to your organization's success as efficiently as possible.

True or false?	
1. Our employees interact well with each other, and we have plenty of opportunities to socialize, collaborate, and learn together.	T / F
2. When our organization is experiencing challenges, the leadership team often solicits feedback or support from staff.	T / F
3. My experience has taught me that some problems are too complicated to solve, and make-do or stop-gap solutions are a less risky way to ensure operational or business stability.	T / F
4. Our organization welcomes new team members and staff but find they often don't stay with us for very long before moving on to their next employment opportunity.	T / F
5. I'm not sure how Veteran skillsets and values will fit into my workplace.	T / F

Consider your answers above. If you responded TRUE to the first two questions and FALSE to the last three questions, Veterans will likely adapt quickly to your workplace.

If your responses differ from the TRUE–TRUE–FALSE–FALSE–FALSE answer key, the *Guide's* activities for attracting and onboarding Veterans will be particularly useful for you and your new Veteran hires.

The name of this assessment—*Will Veteran talent be successful in your organization?*—is a bit of a trick question. Veteran talent is very versatile, and they're eager to find rewarding work. If you provide the tools and structures for them to be successful, they can thrive in any organization.

Understand your Veteran Quotient (VQ)

The business world places a lot of importance on IQ (Intelligence Quotient) as a measurement of someone's likely success in work and life. Over time, a person's EQ (Emotional Quotient) has also come to be accepted as an important indicator of likely success.[1] Personality, social awareness, and the capacity to build relationships all help leaders succeed.

From a career development perspective, EQ is often framed as soft skills, people skills, interpersonal skills, and more. An employee's EQ determines how they work with coworkers, leaders, and clients or customers. It impacts workplace and team dynamics, as well as overall organizational success.

Challenge Factory's research shows that employers who have a higher "Veteran Quotient" (VQ) are more likely to understand how Veterans act in the workplace. They will also have more success in their Veteran hiring efforts and, by extension, their overall hiring success. Improving your VQ can mean the difference between finding a great employee, hiring the wrong employee, or even leaving a position unfilled.

Veteran Quotient (VQ) is a measure of a person's awareness of military Veterans' fit within civilian workplaces.

Career development is the lifelong process of managing learning, work, leisure, and transitions in order to move toward a personally determined and evolving preferred future.

Check out the glossary of military to civilian career transition terms to learn more.

This VQ self-assessment will help you understand how you think about Veterans.

In the following two lists, choose:

- **eight** qualities or characteristics you think Veterans possess or demonstrate

- **eight** qualities or characteristics you think best describes your current workforce

This is your personal opinion, so there are no wrong answers here.

"I think Veterans are…"		"I think my employees are…"	
Ambitious	☐	Ambitious	☐
Determined	☐	Determined	☐
Competitive	☐	Competitive	☐
Decisive	☐	Decisive	☐
Peaceful	☐	Peaceful	☐
Matter of fact	☐	Matter of fact	☐
Patient	☐	Patient	☐
Predictable	☐	Predictable	☐
Eager	☐	Eager	☐
Pressure-oriented	☐	Pressure-oriented	☐
Agreeable	☐	Agreeable	☐
Hesitant	☐	Hesitant	☐
Enthisiastic	☐	Enthisiastic	☐
Persuasive	☐	Persuasive	☐
Suspicious	☐	Suspicious	☐
Careful	☐	Careful	☐
Accurate	☐	Accurate	☐
Openminded	☐	Openminded	☐
Independent	☐	Independent	☐
Uninhibited	☐	Uninhibited	☐

Compare your two lists to see where there are perceived differences between Veterans and your staff.

Did you find it more difficult to see your current workforce as all having the same characteristics? If yes, this may be because you know your employees are all unique people with their own personalities and working styles. The same is true of Veterans.

Also, notice if you are confident that certain characteristics do apply across your entire workforce. This will help you:

- Begin thinking concretely about the type of new hire you would like to bring into your organization.

- Create your Employment Value Proposition (see page 21 of this *Guide*).

The purpose of this VQ self-assessment, like the first self-assessment about Veteran talent fitting into your organization, is meant to get you reflecting about Veterans. Employers often have low Veteran awareness and may possess unintended, unconscious biases about them. This can lead to misperceptions. In most cases, misperceptions skew employers' understandings of how Veterans would behave in and contribute to their organization. Low VQs and unconscious biases can also make employers view Veterans as different from the average civilian in ways they are not.

The best way for employers to improve their VQ score is to gain more direct exposure to Veterans and military communities. Your interest in hiring Veterans and using this *Guide* means you're already on the right track. Keep going and know that the tools in this section are designed to pay off that interest.

> Challenge Factory has done quantitative research to identify the real differences between how employers *think* Veterans act in the workplace and how Veterans *actually* work. See Part 3 for the data findings. See Part 2 to explore the myths about Veterans that need busting.
>
> If you want to know the quantifiable working profile of your workforce (how your employees work individually and as a team), contact us about using our workforce assessment tools today.

Military to civilian translation

Military and civilian culture can seem worlds apart, creating barriers between Veterans and employers who would otherwise benefit from one another. One way to take down these barriers is to focus on looking beyond the language differences. Take the tips, examples, and resources below as a starting point and use them to build your own learning path.

How to approach confusing military jargon — Learning a little can go a long way.		
Translating between military and civilian culture...	During the hiring process...	Remember to...
• isn't always easy • requires patience • shows Veterans that you're invested in them	• don't immediately screen out candidates if their resumes are confusing • prioritize getting to know Veterans as people rather than deciphering their resumes • ask a Veteran employee to help interpret resumes (This may be a future action to remember)	• acknowledge that you'll never have a full understanding of military culture • try not to get frustrated with confusing military language • keep in mind that Veterans may not realize some of their language can be confusing
Learn directly from Veterans whenever possible.		

Sample terminology	
Military	**Civilian**
AAR (After Action Review)	Debrief, lessons learned
Briefing	Meeting
Leave	Time off work
Mission	Goal, task
Pushed to the right	Moved into the future, later than planned
Sitrep (situation report)	Report, update
SOP (Standard Operating Procedures)	Established or routine procedures

Sample resume terminology

Militarized	Demilitarized
Military experience: Corporal in the 48th Highlanders	Professional experience: Five years of junior team leader experience as a Supply Technician in the CAF Primary Reserves
Advanced to the rank of Warrant Officer	Promoted to the position of Department Manager/Head
Commanded an infantry platoon through two successful missions	Supervised a 30-person team in fast-paced, hazardous environments while meeting all organizational goals
Conducted intelligence operations and briefings	Conducted research and analysis, including collating data and presenting findings to supervisors through oral and written reports
Provided structural engineering support to operational units at home and abroad	Worked on construction projects in Canada and Haiti to draft, build, and maintain permanent and temporary structures; duties included surveying, drywalling, framing, masonry, carpentry, etc.

Translation resources

Browse military occupations on the CAF's career website to get a sense of the breadth and diversity of skills, experience, and expertise that Veterans develop during their military careers. The occupation overviews include related civilian occupations.

MNET: Not sure what a Veteran job candidate's role was in the CAF? Not sure which Veterans you should be targeting in your job postings? Use this tool to convert military occupations to their civilian equivalents, or to convert civilian occupations to their military equivalents.

A great resource for more information on translating military to civilian language is Yvonne Rodney's *Military to Civilian Employment: A Career Practitioner's Guide*. In addition to many other topics about Veterans in the workplace, it contains learning about employment and employability, including a militarized and demilitarized resume sample and a comparison of military and civilian occupations.

Lessons learned from hiring managers

"We identified Veterans already working for our organization. When a resume is received from a candidate with a military background, it is redirected to one of our Veteran employees. The Veteran employee then explains the candidate's skills and experiences in civilian terms to the recruiter or hiring manager. As a result, fewer Veteran applications are screened out due to a lack of military understanding."

– Manager, large enterprise, Veteran hiring program

Customize your recruitment materials

Use Veteran Friendly job postings

In your job postings, highlight your interest in hiring Veterans and why they should want to work for you. Veterans do their research on potential employers. Making relevant information about your organization available will be very useful to them. Once you've created content for your website or other marketing materials, it can also be used to create postings or ads on social media platforms and job websites.

The more you show Veterans that you're interested in them as employees and want them to be successful in their civilian lives and careers, the more they'll seek you out. Because there are so many misconceptions, stereotypes, and biases out there about Veterans, simply making your interest visible and explaining that you understand how valuable they are can be incredibly impactful.

Explain why Veterans should want to work at your organization.	Describe your organization's Veteran hiring goals.
Describe your organization's workforce diversity practices or policy.	Profile any Veterans on staff. (This may be a future action to remember.)

ONLINE POSTS	YOUR WEBSITE	PRINTED MATERIALS	OTHER ADS	SOCIAL MEDIA

Check out the Canadian websites of large enterprises for inspiration and examples of how they promote their interest in hiring Veterans. Pay attention to how they advertise careers to Veterans.

ATCO	General Dynamics
BMO	Home Depot
Commissionaires	RBC
FedEx	Scotiabank
GardaWorld	VIA Rail

Create a strong Employment Value Proposition

A key tool that can help you attract the right talent to your organization is the Employment Value Proposition (EVP).

The labour market is exactly that—a market where people buy and sell labour. Like any market, there is a supply side and a demand side. The days of having an endless, ready-made labour supply are largely gone. Demographics, immigration, the COVID-19 pandemic, and the changing nature of work have all impacted labour supply, creating new challenges for finding employees who have the right skills, abilities, and competencies that meet the needs of your organization.

In today's labour market, you can no longer fish with a net. Attracting and retaining the right talent for your organization requires using a hook. To win the competitive search for talent, you have to put as much effort into attracting and retaining employees as you put into landing and keeping customers.

Veterans are a deep, diverse pool of hidden talent who want to work for employers that value them and help them grow. Attracting them to your organization by persuading them why they should work for you will pay dividends. You need a well thought out, strong EVP.

What is your Employment Value Proposition?

Your EVP is the set of attributes that the labour market and your employees perceive as the value they gain by working for your organization. It is a clear, compelling, and distinct description of what employees can expect to experience working for your organization. An EVP helps identify why your organization is attractive and how you differentiate your organization from your competitors. In short, it explains why someone should work for you and what's in it for them when they have many different employment options.

What are the benefits of a strong EVP?[2]

Research has shown that developing a strong EVP has a high return on investment. While it requires putting effort and energy into really understanding your organization, the payoff is worth it. A strong EVP helps organizations:

1. Attract candidates more effectively, especially those who are not actively looking for new work.

2. Decrease compensation costs for new hires. If your EVP is strong, people will want to work for your organization for more than just the money.

3. Drive employee commitment and retention. If what you say about yourself as an organization aligns with who you are, new hires and long-time employees will feel it.

Let's talk culture

Before you can create your EVP, you have to honestly and openly understand your organization's culture. Your organization's culture is a combination of written and unwritten rules, norms, beliefs, behaviours, and values. It is how work gets done, how people interact with each other, and how they see their organization's place in the world.[3]

Think of it this way. Imagine a conversation your employee has at a family dinner. Around the table, your employee's Aunt Jenny asks, "So what's it like working at Company XYZ?" How your employee answers this question is, in essence, your organization's culture.

Does your employee use words like "supportive," "growth," and "dynamic"? Or is it more about "fast," "demanding," and "high rewards"? Or "pressure," "difficult," and "challenging"?

As long as your workplace isn't toxic, unsafe, or dangerous, there is no inherently good or bad culture. Culture is just culture. The secret is understanding your culture and finding talent that fits it well.

Creating your EVP

Once you understand what your culture is truly like, you can begin to define your EVP. A strong EVP includes five components: Rewards, Opportunity, Culture, People, and Work.[4] Within each component, you can consider 38 attributes:

Employment Value Proposition

The set of attributes that the labour market and employees perceive as the value they gain through employment in the organization.

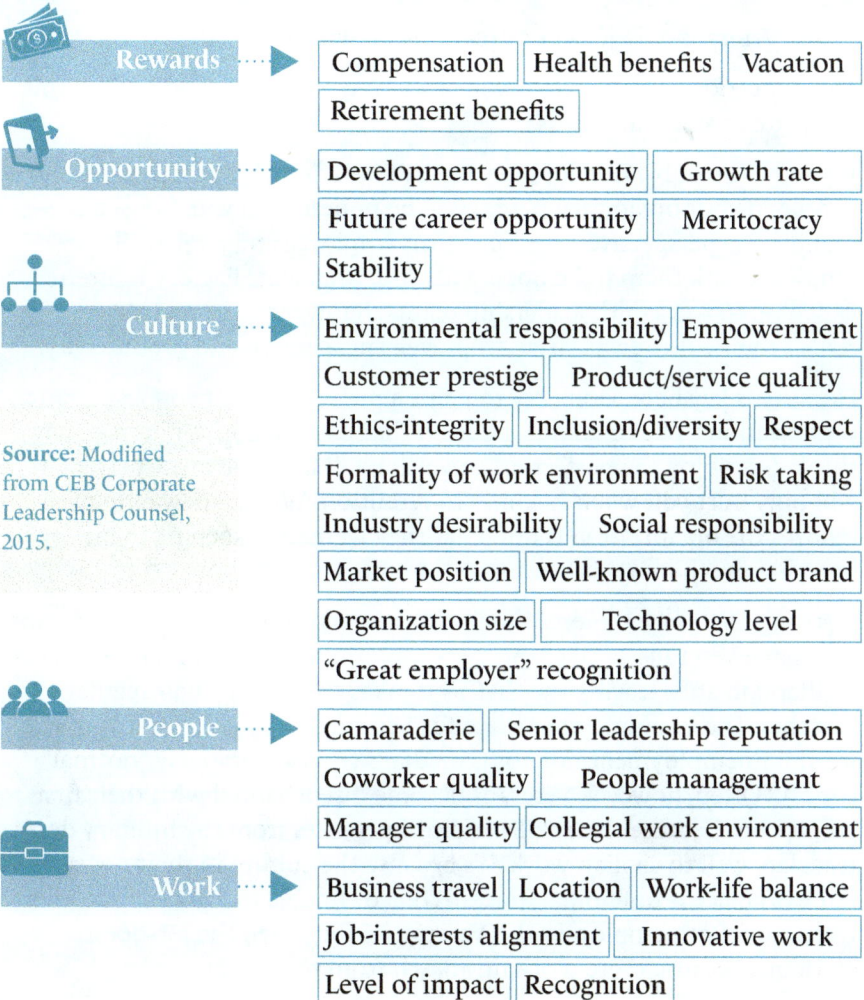

Rewards ····▶ Compensation | Health benefits | Vacation
Retirement benefits

Opportunity ····▶ Development opportunity | Growth rate
Future career opportunity | Meritocracy
Stability

Culture ····▶ Environmental responsibility | Empowerment
Customer prestige | Product/service quality
Ethics-integrity | Inclusion/diversity | Respect
Formality of work environment | Risk taking
Industry desirability | Social responsibility
Market position | Well-known product brand
Organization size | Technology level
"Great employer" recognition

Source: Modified from CEB Corporate Leadership Counsel, 2015.

People ····▶ Camaraderie | Senior leadership reputation
Coworker quality | People management
Manager quality | Collegial work environment

Work ····▶ Business travel | Location | Work-life balance
Job-interests alignment | Innovative work
Level of impact | Recognition

To develop your EVP, finish the following sentences:

1. In our organization, we believe…
2. This belief can be seen in…
3. For those who work here, this means…
4. Evidence that our team/staff would agree with this includes…
5. Compensation here is…
6. Leadership here is…
7. The work here is…
8. Veterans who join our organization will appreciate…

This collection of sentences is your EVP. You can add to and modify this template to suit your needs.

If you have trouble developing your EVP, ask for help. Connect with people in your organization who will be honest with you. Consider seeking the perspectives of a long-term employee and a relatively new employee. Ask them to be open with you. Challenge Factory is often called on to work with leadership teams that want a strong EVP to reflect their culture and drive employee engagement and productivity.

Honesty is key here. Don't try to paint a picture of what you want your organization to be or an organization that you are not. While you may think describing the perfect organization will help you attract talent, it will only hurt you when it comes to retention. When a new employee realizes the organization is not what they were sold, keeping them becomes much more difficult.

A strong EVP is even more valuable for attracting and retaining Veterans. For many Veterans, it takes the same amount of time to find their first civilian job after leaving the CAF as it takes civilians in their regular job searches. The unemployment rate for Veterans is 5%, comparable to the overall unemployment rate for Canadians (in comparatively "normal" times).[5] Often, however, Veterans become disenchanted with their first job. It's not because their skills and competences from the military don't translate well to civilian work. It's because the culture in their new civilian workplace is unfamiliar, unexpected, or unable to fully support their transition. Both employers and Veterans suffer when the job doesn't work out because there was a mismatch from the outset.

By having an EVP that honestly portrays what it is like to work in your organization, Veterans will be better able to judge whether it is the right fit for them. They will take notice if you state explicitly that your organization is a Veteran Friendly Employer or that you welcome Veterans. If you know that the experience of transitioning from the military into the civilian labour market is unique, the Veterans you attract and hire are more likely to want to stay with your organization. The real value in a strong EVP will be Veteran retention.

How to use your EVP

Once you have developed the key points of your EVP, the next step is to share them with your team. Does your perspective on the organization's culture resonate with them? Do they agree it reflects the organization and its culture? Again, encourage your team to be honest with you. This will help you best describe who you are.

When you are comfortable with your EVP, turn it into a narrative that you can share with potential employees. Build your recruitment materials around it, such as your website. Include it in your job postings. Post it on LinkedIn or other social media. Spread your word.

Sample EVPs

1. *In our organization, we believe that compassion, collaboration, and accountability lead to excellence. We believe [Company] is an organization where staff and volunteers can learn and grow.*

   This belief can be seen in the daily work and activities of [Company] staff and volunteers. Compassion is shown to our clients and to each other. Collaboration takes place across the organization from staff huddles, regular meetings, and various communication channels.

   Evidence that our team would agree with this is in the words they choose to describe working at [Company]—compassionate, caring, welcoming, collaborative, and supportive.

   Compensation here is fair.

   Leadership here understands the issues employees face, communicates change and expectations clearly, and provides timely, useful, and constructive feedback.

   The work here is both challenging and rewarding, and all done in a spirit of learning and teamwork.

[Company] is proud to be a Veteran Friendly Employer. We value what Canada's military Veterans can bring to our workplace and are ready to find, hire, welcome, and retain them.

2. *We believe people are not a company's asset, but instead a company's equity. To this end, [Company] helps our clients increase their profitability by investing in their employees and developing their workforces. We do this through research, education, and consulting.*

   Being part of our team means being truly valued as you do meaningful work, learn, and grow. We believe that everyone has exceptional potential to contribute, and they simply need the right space to make it happen. The centre of our culture is being part of our community. [Company] can't help our clients if we are not living our own people-first values.

   If you are a Veteran or Reservist, [Company] would be thrilled to hear from you. We know our workplace benefits from military skillsets and experience, and that transitioning is a process we can be part of for you.

3. *We believe that practicing law is not just knowing about legislation and precedents, but also building relationships and caring about the people we represent.*

   For those who work here, this means working together to create something that we can all be proud of. Our success comes from our people, and we make sure our compensation package reflects this.

   We are a firm where you can grow your practice. More importantly, we are a firm where the partners know you not as a billable entity, but as a real person who has a life inside and outside of work.

   We are a Veteran Ready Employer. Veterans who join our firm will appreciate the opportunity to rise to a range of different challenges, put their transferrable skills to the test, and build a supported, rewarding career.

How to find Veteran jobseekers

There are no shortcuts to finding Veterans who are looking for work. There are, however, targeted steps you can take and supports you can draw on to get to the finish line. Above all, remember:

- Combining recruitment activities that are designed to **attract** the right job candidates with those designed to **find** the right job candidates will lead to better hiring outcomes (compared to only focusing on one or the other type of activity).

- During the recruitment process, stay flexible and positive, embrace trial and error, and adjust your approach as needed.

Look for referrals

Start by asking your current employees if any of them are Veterans or Reservists, or know someone who is. Military and Veteran communities are tightknit and work hard to facilitate job opportunities for each other. They can give you recruitment leads and help spread the word that you are hiring.

When you connect with one person, an entire network will open up to you.

Join VAC's Veteran Employers mailing list

Veterans Affairs Canada (VAC) provides hiring resources and support to its network of Veteran Employers. You have options for how to connect with VAC:

1. Email Hire-Embauchez-Veteran@Veterans.Gc.Ca. In a short message, communicate your interest in hiring Veterans. VAC will be in touch with next steps.

2. Register your organization with VAC by completing the Veteran Employer Registration form.

Join the Hire a Veteran LinkedIn group

The Hire a Veteran/*Embauchez un vétéran* LinkedIn group connects employers, Veterans, and CAF members. Post your job opportunities and learn from other Veteran Friendly and Veteran Ready employers. The group has thousands of members.

Join the LinkedIn group.

Use Job Bank to post jobs

The Government of Canada's Job Bank has a dedicated section for recruiting Veterans. It allows employers to advertise their open positions directly to Veterans. Employers are able to view a list of jobseeker profiles that match the position requirements, and invite matching Veterans to apply with one click.

Visit Job Bank.

Create an account to post a job.

Lessons learned from hiring managers

"We know that finding Veterans requires good relationships with Veterans themselves, their networks, and the units they come from. We make an effort to visit our local base, run job fairs, and attend sessions for CAF members considering transition at the base. We depend on our existing Veterans to guide us to their networks and inform us about the best social media to use to reach the Veteran community. It takes work, but it means we increase our chances of interviewing and hiring great people we might not talk to otherwise."

– Manager, large enterprise, Veteran hiring program

Interviewing Veterans for a job

One of the best ways to learn about Veterans and the military community, to get to know a particular Veteran, or to determine whether they will be a good fit for your organization is to conduct an interview. Interviewing Veterans can sometimes be a bit different than interviewing civilian job candidates.

Use the insights and interview guide below to make small changes to your interview preparation and style so that you can get the most out of meeting with your Veteran candidates. This will also help you improve your interview skills with job candidates who aren't Veterans.

Learn from Lisa: Dig a little deeper

Early on in Challenge Factory's work with Veterans in transition, Lisa Taylor met a remarkable candidate. He was in his early-30s, very charismatic, and in the process of leaving the CAF. She asked the candidate to tell her a bit about himself.

"My name is Trevor," he replied. "I have a high school diploma and I did a bit of woodworking before I joined the military."

Lisa suspected there was much more to the story. After a bit of probing, she learned that Trevor had a medical education and certifications. It also became quite clear that he was one of the best strategists and planners she'd ever met.

Had Lisa taken Trevor's introduction at face value, she likely would have begun exploring possible career paths in the skilled trades with him. Yet all it required to uncover his true talent and passion was asking a few more questions, digging a little bit deeper, and keeping an open mind. Trevor, it turned out, was an expert at navigating complex interpersonal relationships and challenges—and needed a career that reflected this.

The Veteran interview experience

A little empathy goes a long way. Here's what you need to know to understand, relate to, and empathize with Veterans—and your other job candidates.

Veterans will be nervous.

- Nervousness may clash with stereotypical portrayals of Veterans in popular culture. Don't let this impact your first impression of them.

Veterans may be out of their element.

- Job interviews are different in the military. A Veteran may have never gone on a civilian interview before.

Veterans may want:

- Cues from you about the authority and formality dynamics at play in the interview
- Clarity on the interview process and questions

Don't let Veterans downplay their successes.

Your Veteran job candidate will not be used to openly discussing their own strengths, successes, or capabilities. They're trained not to put themselves at the centre of any success, even when they made a significant contribution to it—and when it's in their best interest to disclose their contribution.

If your candidate appears to be minimizing their military work, or struggling to share career highlights, rephrase your question. Instead, ask about a meaningful experience that made them proud of the work being done. Then, use their story to drill into the specific role they played in that experience.

Make sure Veterans discuss their military experience.

Veterans may assume that civilian employers are aware of the occupations in the military, and what their own occupation entailed. As a result, they may think you don't want to hear specific details about their military work. They may also think the questions you ask about their work history only pertain to their civilian experiences. For example, you may find someone with 20 years of military experience sharing a story about a summer job they had in high school.

Give Veterans clear opportunities to speak about their work in the military, and make sure they know you need to hear about it to properly assess them as a job candidate.

Find Veterans' business acumen beneath military-civilian language mismatches.

Veterans may not be familiar with certain business terms, even if their military occupation saw them working on similar activities. For example, "marketing" or "CFO" may not be terms that they used in their day-to-day military work. Rest assured, however, that military experience requires smart and persuasive communication, as well as strong asset management and acumen.

Public relations and customer/client relations are important components of many military occupations. Recruiters "sell" the CAF as a viable employment choice. Soldiers in combat and support roles rely on community relations, build relationships with vendors and service providers, conduct targeted research, and so on. Veterans don't lack the skills behind these common business terms; they just call them by different names. During the interview, bridge those gaps between Veterans' business acumen and the language you use to talk about it.

Focus on Veterans' interview preparation.

Expect the job candidate to be well prepared. Ask them specifically how they prepared for the interview. This is a practical way of evaluating how they seek information, create their own plan, identify key resources, and support themselves.

Lay out the next steps clearly.

Be clear about the hiring process. Describe what happens next, when the job candidate can expect to hear back from you, and who they should contact if they have additional questions or follow-up.

Onboarding new Veteran hires

Onboarding new hires the right way, whether or not they are Veterans, is key to long-term retention. Having a clear onboarding process helps you build employee engagement, workplace integration and connection, and productivity from their very first day. The onboarding framework provided below gives you a strong foundation for building and implementing a complete onboarding process.

Why use an onboarding framework?

1 Establishes a foundation for a strong working relationship

2 Prepares new hires for personal and organizational success

3 Sets out specific activities and timeframes

4 Provides structure and clarity to both employer and employee

5 Veterans will expect it—they come from a highly formalized, regimented environment

Don't have a complete, formal onboarding process yet? Consider enlisting the first Veteran you hire to create or document useful tools and templates based on their own onboarding experience. Regardless of their role and rank in the military, they've been trained to add this type of value to the organization they work for—and they're well-suited to the task.

Challenge Factory's work with business owners, leaders, and hiring managers focuses on the direct links between healthy employee careers and organizational success. Check out our action-focused *Retain and Gain* series of career management playbooks (for small businesses, nonprofits and charities, and the public sector) to access over 40 activities that employers can do with their employees to ensure continued career growth and happy workforces.

Lessons learned from hiring managers

"When we bring in a new Veteran, we make sure they have a buddy for the first few months. The buddy isn't necessarily someone they work with every day. This is someone who can answer questions that are confusing to a newly released Veteran, such as:

- 'How do I apply for health benefits?'
- 'How do I deal with unionized employees?'
- 'How do I communicate with other employees who don't seem to understand me?'

We think of the buddy system as a leadership development opportunity for staff members, and we recognize them for this work."

– Manager, large enterprise, Veteran hiring program

Framework for onboarding Veterans

This framework can be built on and adapted to suit your unique needs.

Step 1: Before the first day

Goal: Ensure the organization and new employee are ready for a good start.

Questions for the employer

- What resources will the new employee require to do their job?

- Has the new employee's direct supervisor learned about military experience? (They may benefit from exploring *The Canadian Guide to Hiring Veterans*.)

- Is it clear how the new employee's role/work will contribute to the success of the organization?

- Who are ten people (i.e., staff, managers, partners, clients, etc.) the new employee should meet in their first three weeks on the job?

- Can you assign someone within the organization to be your new employee's "work buddy" (coach, guide, support) during the onboarding process?

Questions for the new employee to consider before their first day

- What questions do you have about this new role, work environment, chain of command, and expectations (for you and your employer)?

- What might you learn, do, and teach others in this role?

- What information, introductions, tools, and skills do you think you'll need (that you may not currently have)?

Step 2: On the first day

Goal: Create a good first impression and working relationship.

Activities for the employer

- Be prepared to meet your new employee at the time you specified. Anticipate that they will arrive a few minutes early.

- Provide an agenda for the new employee's first day. This should outline how their time will be spent. Include time-blocks for an office or location tour (if appropriate), a coffee break with team members, a session to complete paperwork, lunch with their direct supervisor, and an opportunity to get any equipment set up (e.g., email, software, workspace, etc.).

- Spend time reviewing formal workplace policies. Ensure the new employee understands the formal and informal rules of how your organization operates.

- Schedule a time to review the new employee's learning and work goals. Ask what they want to learn, do, and teach others in the next six months.

Goal: Get the new employee engaged and productive as quickly as possible.

Activities for the employer and employee together

- Set up and complete any required training (e.g., compliance, safety, job-related, etc.).

- Connect the new employee with their "work buddy" and ensure regular meetings are set up.

- Ensure the new employee knows they can ask questions, and ask them questions as well. In this way, the new employee can fill the gaps in their knowledge and you can mine the value of having a talented set of fresh eyes on your organization's operations.

- Ensure the new employee is busy. Provide ample work that accurately reflects their role and duties. It's important that the new employee learns quickly what they'll need to do to be successful.

- Ensure the new employee meets a new (and different) contact each day. This meeting doesn't have to be long or formal, but the new employee should have opportunities to meet with the people identified in Step 1 during their first three weeks on the job. Remember to also provide opportunities for the new employee and "work buddy" to connect regularly during these first crucial weeks.

Goal: Revisit your onboarding process to see if any changes are needed.

Activities for the employer

Even when you have a strong onboarding process in place, new information and market conditions may require you to make a change. After a period of high volume hiring or at least once a year, gather feedback about your onboarding process by asking your hiring managers (if you have them) and newest employees the following questions. You can send them in an email, create a survey, or set up a one-on-one or group meeting. Choose the method that will best fit your culture.

Questions for the employer/hiring managers only

1. Knowing what you know now, would you change the order, urgency, or supports used during the first three months of a new hire's employment?

Questions for both the employer/hiring managers and new employees

1. What do you remember about the onboarding experience that was challenging?

2. What do you remember about the onboarding experience that was critical to your success?

3. In reviewing the Employment Value Proposition (EVP) for our organization, has the experience of the first three months within the organization lived up to the culture described? If not, why not?

As you review the answers your receive, consider the following: What positive work surprises do any Veteran employees think should have been described upfront? How have the hiring managers used your EVP to guide discussions and decision-making?

PART 2 | HIRING SCENARIOS THAT BUST MYTHS ABOUT VETERANS

The best way to understand the value of Veterans as a hidden talent pool is to learn more about them as real people—rather than as abstract representations. This means becoming aware of myths about Veterans that are common in our society.

Where do myths about Veterans come from?

- Myths come from misconceptions, stereotypes, and biases about Veterans.

- They may inaccurately represent Veterans' abilities, experiences, or characteristics.

- Many myths are perpetuated in television, movies, and other pop culture media.

- Other myths are subtler and take more effort to become aware of—in the workplace, for example.

These myths affect every Veteran at some point in their post-military life. They occur at the broader level of Canada's cultural landscape, across workplaces that would benefit from employing Veterans, and within civilians who only need to shift their thinking a little. For employers, making this mindset shift will help unlock a talent pool of ready and eager jobseekers.

In this section, we present nine myths about Veterans in the workplace that often prevent employers from considering them as suitable candidates. Each myth is presented through a hiring scenario, with a fictional Veteran character and employer character who meet and go through the hiring and onboarding process together. The scenario provides details about the Veteran, why the employer hires them, what the employer does to retain them, and what the outcome of the employer's hiring decision is. Because more than one myth can affect a Veteran or employer at the same time, you may be able to find additional myths in each scenario on top of the main myth that is being spotlighted.

The use of scenarios and characters to bust myths builds on Challenge Factory's expertise in using personas and storytelling. By placing both people and evidence-based research at the centre of our workforce solutions, we ground abstract data and statistics in real-life experiences and create empathy and connections between humans. This helps business owners and other leaders make informed decisions and build better workplaces.

Lessons learned from hiring managers

"We work hard to bust myths about Veterans. We know Veterans are not all the same, and we know they've had careers in a unique environment that we civilians don't necessarily understand or relate to. We encourage learning sessions where Veterans can answer questions about military life and culture. This makes our organization stronger—and our Veterans get to understand some of the contrasts between where they've come from and how our organization operates."

– **Manager, large enterprise, Veteran hiring program**

Hiring scenario 1 – The health myth

Myth: Veterans are all injured or unhealthy.

Vijay – Veteran

Reason for leaving the CAF: Medical

Salary in the last year of military service: $58,700

Military occupation: Materiel Management Technician

Civilian job after service: Shipping and Receiving Clerk

Hilary – Hiring Manager

Civilian employer that hires Vijay: Mid-sized manufacturing company

Reasons for hiring Vijay: Vijay would not be the first member of Hilary's team to have a health challenge. She knows it doesn't matter if one or all of her team members has a medical issue. As a manager, she needs to know how to support them all.

Hiring outcome

- Vijay impresses Hilary and his peers during his onboarding and quickly becomes a valued member of the team.
- In his first three months on the job, Vijay accesses available supports for all new employees and doesn't raise any issues with Hilary that require additional accommodation.
- Vijay becomes a strong peer supporter to others on the team who are struggling. In the CAF, he was trained as a peer supporter.

Busting the myth

Sometimes Veterans like Vijay are viewed as a hiring risk because it's assumed they have physical or mental health challenges, which may make them less employable. But physical and mental health challenges are not Veteran- or military-specific.

Just over 1 in 4 Canadians (27%) aged 15 years and older, or 8.0 million people, have a disability that limits them in their daily activities.[6]

Many Veterans leave the military in good health. In 2019, 65% of CAF members left the military voluntarily, and 31% left for medical reasons.[7]

There's no reason to downplay the traumatic effects that armed conflict can have on soldiers. But assuming every Veteran has a health challenge leads to missed employment opportunities for both jobseekers and employers.

No two Veterans are the same, and you should approach their health in the same way you approach your civilian employees' health.

Hiring scenario 2 – The education myth

Myth: Veterans are less educated and only look for entry-level jobs.

Paulina – Veteran

Reason for leaving the CAF: Family decision after 12 years of service

Military rank group at end of service: Senior Non-Commissioned Member (NCM)

Military occupation: Marine Technician

Salary in the last year of military service: $72,280

Education: College degree

Civilian job after service: Partnership Development Coordinator

Malik – Start-up founder

Civilian employer that hires Paulina: Start-up in marine innovation

Reasons for hiring Paulina: During their interview, Malik realizes Paulina is very charismatic and excels at building relationships. Instead of hiring her as a Marine Equipment Electrician, Malik offers her a Partnership Development Coordinator role, where Paulina will cultivate and manage strategic partnerships with organizations, businesses, government, and other interest holders across the marine industry.

Hiring outcome

- Paulina thrives at Malik's start-up and stays long-term.
- Later, Paulina becomes an integral member of Malik's leadership team.

Busting the myth

Veterans like Paulina don't want to be stuck in entry-level jobs. Why would they when they're so highly trained? Veterans want to build long-term careers that make use of their skills and experience and continue their professional growth.

Many Veterans get post-secondary educations as well as their military training. Paulina's college degree was paid for by the CAF.

If you're looking for job candidates who have completed college, CEGEP, or a trade certificate, Veterans are more likely than the general population to meet this criteria.[8] If a Veteran Officer applies for a job with you, they are more likely to have a higher education than your civilian candidates.[9]

Veterans have varying levels of education, just like the general population. Each job candidate should be evaluated on their own merits.

Regardless of traditional education, Veterans develop transferrable skills that are tested and earned in extreme conditions where irresponsibility and failure can mean real lives lost.

Hiring scenario 3 – The drill sergeant myth

Myth: Veterans are all take-charge people who want to be in control and give orders.

Antonio – Veteran

Military occupation: Special Forces Operator

Civilian job after service: Risk Analyst

Reason for applying to current position: Antonio is not interested in managing people. Instead, he wants a job where he can be part of a supportive team and apply his expertise in analyzing complex situations and identifying, assessing, and mitigating risks that could impact the financial health and stability of his employer and their clients.

Dennis – HR Advisor

Civilian employer that hires Antonio: Financial services company

Dennis' first impressions of Antonio: During their interview, Dennis is surprised to discover that Antonio is soft-spoken, laidback, charming, and not physically imposing. Antonio is not what Dennis pictured a Special Forces Operator to be. His qualifications for the risk management position that needs to be filled are exemplary.

Hiring outcome

- Antonio quickly builds strong relationships with his colleagues, learns his new role quickly and performs well, and becomes known as the "funny guy" in the office.
- Antonio and the company's Chief Risk Officer develop a mentorship that helps Antonio become a specialist in his civilian field.

Busting the myth

Many Canadians develop their perceptions of Veterans from what they see in American television and movies. Veterans encompass a diverse range of personalities and leadership styles. Some possess strong leadership qualities and prefer to take charge, while others excel in collaborative environments, adapt to a variety of team and leadership roles, and demonstrate flexibility in their approach to teamwork and decision-making.

All military training emphasizes learning how to solve problems, work with discipline, and integrate into a team. Like most employees, they work well with good leadership, direction, and mentoring.

Check out Challenge Factory's research on how Veterans act in the workplace (Part 3).

Hiring scenario 4 – The failure-to-adapt myth

Myth: Veterans are unable to adapt to civilian work.

Lee – Veteran

Military occupation: Infantry Officer

Civilian job after service: Communications Coordinator

Reason for applying to current position: Even though the job posting is filled with unfamiliar civilian language and corporate-speak, Lee wants to pursue a career in Public Relations and knows his experience in leading teams, planning, training, intelligence, logistics, and personnel administration will serve him and a civilian employer well. He's confident he can adapt to a civilian workplace by using his military experience working in high-pressure environments around the world. Now, he just has to get through the job application process.

Renata – Director of Public Relations

Civilian employer that hires Lee: Large enterprise in the automotive industry

What Renata does to hire great talent like Lee: At first, Renata finds Lee's resume confusing because it uses unfamiliar military jargon. She spends ten minutes consulting military-to-civilian translation guides, then decides to invite Lee for an interview. During the interview, Renata discovers that Lee's military skills will be an asset to their company, especially his attention to detail, quick-thinking, flexibility in problem solving, and skills in crisis management, strategic planning, and interacting with a range of interest holders.

Hiring outcome

- During Lee's onboarding, Renata pairs him with a "work buddy" who can answer questions about their workplace.
- Lee has all the resources he needs to adapt to his new civilian work. When he makes a mistake, he takes responsibility and learns from it.
- As Lee grows into his role, he becomes a "work buddy" and mentor to new hires.

Busting the myth

In some ways, Veterans are like newcomers and immigrants. They face many of the same challenges when it comes to finding employment in an unfamiliar marketplace and work environment. When Lee enters the civilian job market and begins his first civilian job, he feels like he's entering foreign territory—as he did on deployment in the military.

Veterans have diverse and valuable skills, but it takes effort to translate them to civilian work environments. This translation can feel like learning a new language. This doesn't mean Veterans are incapable of adapting to civilian work. An important part of military training is learning how to adapt to different and unfamiliar environments. All they need is support, just like anyone else who's beginning a new job.

Hiring scenario 5 – The civilian work awareness myth

Myth: Veterans always understand civilian employment conditions and expectations.

Neil – Veteran

Reason for leaving the CAF: Needs to be available to care for his ailing father

Military occupation: Imagery Technician

Civilian job after service: Social Media Manager

Transition challenge: When he leaves the CAF, Neil begins providing care for his father and struggles with working 9:00 AM to 5:00 PM. Instead of bringing this to his boss' attention, Neil does everything he can on his own to make those hours work. Neil is also unfamiliar with what's included in the competitive benefits package he receives, and if it is valuable for his family's situation. Because of these practical uncertainties and struggles, Neil considers leaving his first civilian job after only a couple months.

Francis – Executive Director

Civilian employer that hires Neil: Non-profit organization

What Francis does to retain great talent like Neil: Francis' brother was in the CAF, so he knows that working in a civilian workplace for the first time can be a challenge for Veterans. His brother didn't know basic aspects about civilian work life, like that his new colleagues didn't work on weekends. As part of the onboarding process, Francis shares information with Neil about the practicalities of working for his organization that he wouldn't state explicitly to other new hires.

Hiring outcome

- Because Francis intentionally made sure Neil knows he can ask questions, Neil realizes he can ask for support in learning about unfamiliar civilian employment conditions.
- Francis allows Neil to work 8:30 AM to 4:30 PM, which helps Neil balance work and family responsibilities.
- Neil remains with the company and Francis avoids having to go through another costly hiring process.
- Over time, Neil becomes a resource that other new hires turn to for help understanding the organization's competitive benefits packages.

Busting the myth

Civilian life and employment can be very unfamiliar to Veterans. More than half of Regular Force Veterans (54%) serve in the CAF for more than 20 years.[10] This means many Veterans like Neil aren't returning to the civilian job market, but instead entering it for the first time in decades—or ever.

Many Veterans like Neil also know little about civilian healthcare plans and other benefits, employment contracts, resume writing, and job searches. They have to learn about employment conditions that civilians tend to take for granted. This can make them appear to be a less suitable hiring choice, when in reality they may be perfect for the position.

Hiring scenario 6 – The easy-to-identify myth

Myth: Veterans are easy to identify.

Adam – Veteran

Reason for leaving the CAF: Medical

Military occupation: Signal Operator

Civilian job after service: Information Systems Analyst

Transition challenge: Adam finds the transition to civilian life overwhelming. His identity is closely tied to his military service, but he doesn't disclose that he's a Veteran during most of his civilian job search. This makes him feel even more isolated and disconnected from his identity. In one cover letter, though, Adam decides to share that he's a Veteran.

Ashley – Small business owner

Civilian employer that hires Adam: Software development company

What Ashley does to hire great talent like Adam: When Ashley reads Adam's job application, she notices that although Adam says he's a Veteran, there's very little detail about his military experience on his resume.

Ashley is also uncertain about hiring Adam because she's never worked with a Veteran. Ashley asks her team if any of them have worked with a Veteran. She's very surprised to discover that two staff members also have military backgrounds and one staff member is a part-time Reservist in the Navy.

Hiring outcome

- Adam works diligently to put the knowledge he gained in the CAF about communications and information systems to good use in his new civilian job.
- Adam gets the training he needs and his new colleagues—civilians, Veterans, and Reservist—help him adjust to a post-military work life.
- Ashley gains new confidence in her hiring decisions.

Busting the myth

Veterans like Adam look just like anyone else. They may not self-identify for fear of being judged. You've probably met Veterans without even knowing it.

Because Veterans are typically not easy to identify, the challenges they face can also go unnoticed:

- The loss of their military culture and identity
- Unfamiliar civilian work situations (civilian job searches, workplaces, benefits packages, etc.)
- New personal life experiences (changing family dynamics, relocation, finances, healthcare plans, etc.)
- A long and complicated administrative process to leave the military (making them eager for a straightforward civilian job search)
- Overloaded Veteran support programs and services
- The need to tackle multiple challenges at the same time

Imagine trying to nail a job interview on top of juggling all these challenges and the emotions that come with them (e.g., apprehension, confusion, isolation, uncertainty, and more).

As with the general population, helping Veterans find quality, stable employment can improve their overall quality of life. This can be incredibly important for transitioning Veterans who are struggling with the loss of their military identity and support structures.[11]

Hiring scenario 7 – The identical Veterans myth

Myth: Veterans are all the same.

Julian – Veteran

Military occupation: Training Development Officer

Civilian job after service: e-Learning Specialist

Reason for applying to current position: Julian reads the Employment Value Proposition (EVP) included in a job posting at a university, including what it's like to work there. He had never considered applying for jobs in post-secondary education because he feels like it would be more unfamiliar than a private sector workplace. But based on the EVP's description of the university department's culture and values, Julian thinks it might be a good fit for him.

Mei – Department Administrator

Civilian employer that hires Julian: Post-secondary institution

What Mei does to hire great talent like Julian: Mei hired a Veteran in the past, and he didn't stay in his job for long. As a result, she believes that Veterans aren't a good talent pool to draw from.

Mei has struggled to find and retain great talent in the past, and decides to develop an EVP for the university department she works for. She includes the EVP in her job postings and begins to see stronger candidates, both civilians and Veterans like Julian, when there's a role to fill.

During the hiring and onboarding process, Julian stands out from the other applicants and Mei realizes she had created a stereotype in her mind about Veterans based on an experience with one person.

THE CANADIAN GUIDE TO HIRING VETERANS

Hiring outcome

- Julian excels in his role and discovers a passion for e-Learning and the post-secondary education sector.
- Mei adds a Veteran Friendly Employer component to the university department's EVP, and she begins to notice more Veterans applying to job openings.
- The department's senior leadership team recognizes the value of having an EVP and uses it during other decision-making, strategic planning, and workforce development activities.

Busting the myth

There's no typical Veteran. One Veteran should not be typecast based on another—or based on a stereotype. Like newcomers and immigrants, Veterans can be subconsciously treated as representative of the entire Veteran population.

Veterans all have different work histories, military experiences, and transitions to civilian life. Just like civilians, some Veterans make better employees than others. They should be assessed on their own merits, not their Veteran identity.

Hiring scenario 8 – The military skills myth

Myth: It's too hard to determine how a Veteran fits into a business role.

Military occupation: Bioscience Officer

Education: Graduate studies in occupational health

Civilian job after service: Vice President of Health, Safety, and Environment

Sebastien – Senior HR Manager

Civilian employer that hires Rachel: Engineering and architecture firm

What Sebastien does to hire great talent like Rachel: When a trusted member of Sebastien's professional network recommends Rachel for the Vice President role he needs to fill, Sebastien suspects she won't have the right qualifications or experience. Sebastien doesn't know what a Bioscience Officer does in the military, Rachel has never worked in the engineering and architecture industry, and none of the keywords he looks for in applicants' resumes are present in her resume.

But instead of fixating on the lack of a complete match between Rachel's military job title and the job title he's hiring for, Sebastien meets with Rachel and focuses on learning about her individual agency, motivations, and competencies.

Hiring outcome

- Sebastien and the rest of the firm's leadership team realize that bringing Rachel on board will be well worth the effort.
- Rachel's training in a new industry goes smoothly because of her strong transferrable skills, ambition, and goal-oriented approach to her work.

Busting the myth

Veterans like Rachel are often guided into civilian careers that seem superficially similar to military service (such as security work), without recognizing the breadth and variety of occupations in the military.

There's no one-to-one fit between military and business roles. But many Veterans thrive in business positions. Military roles, like those in civilian life, change and evolve constantly. Although some military occupations can be very specialized, the attributes that make a CAF member successful are the same that make a civilian successful (critical thinking, problem solving, perseverance, team-work, leadership, etc.).

Understanding military occupations can help you find a suitable job candidate, but it will be more useful to focus on how Veterans can be trained within your organization. Veterans' transferrable skills are their most valuable asset.

Veterans can be ambitious, and they've all received intensive military training. They're capable of developing professionally and progressing within an organization.

Hiring scenario 9 – The military culture myth

Myth: Cultures and practices found in military and business environments are too different.

Reason for leaving the CAF: Retirement after 25 years of service

Military rank group at end of service: Officer

Salary in the last year of military service: $89,580

Education: University degree

Civilian self-employment after service: Leadership consultant

Reason for pursuing civilian work: For some Veterans like Émilie, exploring civilian career opportunities is about finding work they're passionate about rather than jumping at the first offer to come their way. Émilie knows that the decades of leadership experience she gained in the military can help leaders in civilian workplaces.

Sahar – CEO

Reason for hiring Émilie as a consultant: Sahar's large company needs help tackling a range of business and workforce challenges. She decides to hire a leadership consultant.

Sahar's first impressions of Émilie: At first, Sahar is skeptical Émilie will be able to help her leadership team grow and tackle tough challenges, especially since Émilie has only just hung out her consultant shingle.

Hiring outcome

- Sahar quickly gains an appreciation for Émilie's deep understanding of people and the skills, knowledge, and mindset a leader needs, regardless of what environment they work in.
- Émilie uses the similarities and differences between military and business environments to provide new perspective, clarity of purpose, and unique ways of thinking about Sahar's business and workforce challenges.

Busting the myth

There *are* differences between military and business environments:

- Military culture comes with very specific practices, behaviours, and language.
- Rank structure in the military is different than organizational structure in business.
- The goals in military and business environments can be very different and emphasize different values.
- Although the majority of CAF members work in office settings, military training also comes with fieldwork.

But there are also important similarities between military and business environments:

- Focus on a common goal
- Need for leaders, teamwork, and initiative
- Presence of competition
- Clearly defined hierarchical structure
- Office setting

PART 3 | DATA-INFORMED HIRING APPROACHES: MEASURING THE HIDDEN TALENT ADVANTAGE

This *Guide* has given you tools and learning to help you:

1. Attract, find, hire, and retain Veterans (Part 1)

2. Bust myths about Veterans in the workplace so you understand the true value of this hidden talent pool (Part 2)

Part 3 explores in more detail why becoming a Veteran Friendly Employer is a worthwhile strategy. This section draws on the results of Challenge Factory's quantitative research that has measured the effectiveness of Veteran hiring resources and how Veterans really act in the workplace. It shows that when employers use hiring skills and HR approaches that focus on Canada's military Veterans, they also improve their overall hiring, HR processes, work culture, and career management.

As a hidden talent pool, the business advantage that Veterans bring to organizations of all types is real. Amidst tight labour markets that feel like they are constantly changing and growing more complex, prioritizing solutions to your hiring and retention challenges that are informed by credible, reliable data can make all the difference. Having sound data findings that you can depend on will not only increase the quality of your decision-making, but also make you more confident in yourself during the process.

Take the *Guide*'s short self-assessment to determine your level of awareness of military Veterans' fit within civilian workplaces. This is your **Veteran Quotient (VQ)**.

> ### Lessons learned from hiring managers
>
> "We know Veterans moved through multiple roles in their CAF careers, and they like the variety and learning that comes with that movement. We have a development plan in our organization that allows Veterans to move through different projects and roles so they can learn about the company and find the role that fits them best."
>
> – **Manager, large enterprise, Veteran hiring program**

Do Veteran hiring resources really help employers?

The short answer is **yes.**

When small organizations become Veteran Friendly Employers, they improve not only their Veteran hiring skills, but also their overall skills in hiring, onboarding, and retaining the right talented employees (both Veterans and non-Veterans). Larger enterprises also benefit from considering how their current practices help or disadvantage Veterans as part of broader DEI awareness and consideration for all candidates and employees.

Challenge Factory has three resources that are designed to help employers hire and retain Veterans:

1. *The Canadian Guide to Hiring Veterans*
2. MasterClass in Hiring: Tap into the Hidden Talent Pool of Canada's Veterans
3. Hidden Talent: A Challenge Factory Podcast

We tested how useful employers found our Veteran hiring resources. We recruited business owners, organization leaders, and hiring managers across Canada to explore the resources and help us assess their impact over a six-month period.

> Here's everything you need to know about Challenge Factory's three research-backed Veteran hiring resources.

Here's what our national impact study found:

1. Veteran hiring resources change how employers think about Veterans.

This shows that quality employer-focused tools can lead to positive Veteran hiring outcomes and stronger overall recruitment and retention practices.

2. Employers made real changes to their hiring practices after exploring a Veteran hiring resource.

- Immediately after exploring a resource, 62% of employers planned to create or update their employee onboarding process.

- Three months after exploring a resource, 55% of employers had changed how they attract and seek out talent.

- Six months after exploring a resource, another 43% of employers had changed how they attract and seek out talent, and 34% had upgraded their onboarding process.

At the end of six months, more than two dozen employers had hired 205 people, including 25 Veterans.

3. Using Veteran hiring resources helps employers build their overall confidence in hiring.

After exploring the resources, employers described feeling empowered, engaged, better informed, inspired, intrigued, ready to investigate the possibility of hiring Veterans, interested in considering Veteran status during hiring decisions, and more.

Using resources that help employers hire Veterans also makes their overall HR work easier and better. For example, creating an EVP is useful for attracting quality job candidates of all types, not just Veterans. Having a Veteran hiring strategy and an EVP shifts employers' focus to building strong work cultures, which plays a significant role in attracting and retaining the right people.

Explore more results of the national impact study.

- Infographic about shifts in employer perceptions of Veterans

- Infographic about the confidence levels that employers experience over six months after using a resource

Fast facts about the impact of Veteran hiring resources

According to employers, *The Canadian Guide to Hiring Veterans* helps them better understand:

Hidden talent pools	**92%**
Canada's military Veterans	**88%**
Career management	**77%**

A majority of employers:

- Spend about an hour exploring *The Canadian Guide to Hiring Veterans*

- Prefer to use a combination of a course resource (MasterClass in Hiring) and a book resource (*The Canadian Guide to Hiring Veterans*) to improve their hiring

After using a Veteran hiring resource:

85% of employers are very likely to consider hiring Veterans to fill their labour or skills gaps.

89% of employers are very likely to consider hiring a job candidate if they find out they're a Veteran.

> ## Lessons learned from hiring managers
>
> "When our organization got really serious about hiring ex-military candidates, we appointed a Veteran to lead the hiring program. He created a campaign to build relationships with local bases and attended education sessions at them to answer questions and make the case for why we were a great employer for Veterans and Reservists. He also became the main contact person for people who were being considered as hires. Then, once they joined us, he mentored them for the first year; they could call him anytime and ask for advice and guidance. As we hired more Veterans, he trained some of them to be mentors."
>
> **– Manager, large enterprise, Veteran hiring program**

How Veterans act in the workplace

An important part of becoming a Veteran Friendly Employer is learning the difference between how employers may *think* Veterans act in the workplace (e.g., their behaviours, personalities, and values), and how they *actually* act.

We've done first-of-its-kind quantitative research that compares how Veterans and civilians work, and what employers think about them.

Takeaways from the data findings

- Veterans have a unique "working profile" that differs from the Canadian norm. This means there are differences in the ways that Veterans and civilians act in the workplace.

- Employers do have perceptions of Veterans that don't accurately reflect how they actually work.

- The Veteran working profile demonstrates that Veterans can succeed in a wide range of employment roles. This means employers can and should consider Veterans for a wide range of jobs and professional advancement.

- Employers who have served in the CAF, or have a direct family member who has served, are more likely to have a clear understanding of how Veterans work.

The employer's assumption

Veterans have a more take-charge, aggressive approach to their communication than civilians.

The truth

Veterans are no more take-charge and aggressive when communicating than the average Canadian.

The result of the assumption

Employers may wrongly assume that Veterans who act more passive and collaborative are uncertain of themselves or less competent.

What you should know about the Veteran working profile

A "working profile" refers to how someone typically works. There are always exceptions to the rule, but, overall, the following profile provides an accurate representation of how Veterans act, behave, think, and approach work.

This working profile has been developed using rigorously tested quantitative research methods.

Compared to the average Canadian, Veterans are actually…

…more curious and receptive.

Veterans are driven by opportunities to learn and gain new knowledge. They don't only rely on their own instincts and intuition, but instead actively pursue new ideas, methods, and opportunities.

…more innovative and flexible.

Veterans aren't always sticklers for traditional, proven methods. They're willing to embrace innovative, novel approaches that differ from long-established systems and structures already in place.

…less commanding and more collaborative.

Veterans enjoy being in supporting roles and don't demand recognition for their individual contributions. They're not driven by status and control, and they welcome the opinions and perspectives of others.

…better critical thinkers and problem solvers.

Veterans are adept at thinking critically and solving problems—in both practical, hands-on situations and structural, theory-based situations.

Our research also shows that employers have some common misperceptions about the Veteran working profile. These misperceptions can lead to missed opportunities between employers and Veteran jobseekers.

Employers often believe that Veterans are...

...less curious and receptive than they really are.

Employers can inaccurately believe that Veterans rely too much on their own instincts and intuition, rather than making an effort to learn and acquire new knowledge. They're perceived as less likely to pursue new ideas, methods, and opportunities. As a result, they may seem interested in new knowledge only when the need arises.

...less innovative and flexible than they really are.

Employers can inaccurately believe that Veterans are sticklers for traditional, proven methods. This makes them seem less willing to embrace innovative, novel approaches that differ from the long-established systems and structures already in place.

...more commanding and less collaborative than they really are.

Employers can inaccurately believe that Veterans always like to take charge, and prioritize their own individuality over others. This makes them seem less willing to take on supporting roles, and less adept at building rapport with coworkers and customers. They're also perceived as placing a lot of importance on status, control, and recognition.

...poorer critical thinkers and problem solvers than they really are.

Employers can inaccurately believe that Veterans struggle to think critically and solve structural or theory-based problems.

...less grounded and calm than they really are.

Employers can inaccurately believe Veterans to be less stable, steady, consistent, and predictable. This makes them seem more active, restless, impatient, and impulsive. They're also viewed as not prioritizing personal change and growth.

Lessons learned from hiring managers

"We consider Veterans a valuable talent pool that's often over-looked in the business community. They're highly trained and have highly developed characteristics, such as teamwork, leadership, and problem solving. When we hire Veterans, we tend to look beyond their technical skills unless they're a match for a specific position that we're filling. Instead, we turn the thinking upside down. We want to know about the Veteran's leadership capability, planning skills, and interpersonal ability. We want to start with these characteristics and then figure out what specific skills the new hire needs."

– Manager, large enterprise, Veteran hiring program

PART 4 | RESOURCES

Attention to our print readers

In the digital version of *The Canadian Guide to Hiring Veterans*, the green-coloured text is clickable, opening websites or jumping to other sections within the publication. For full access to this feature of the *Guide*, download your free digital copy at www.ChallengeFactory.ca/VeteranHiringGuide.

Becoming a better employer for military Veterans will help you become a better employer overall. Unlike much of the general Canadian population, Veterans have their own targeted support eco-system, which you can tap into as well. Part 4 collects and organizes all the resources referenced throughout *The Canadian Guide to Hiring Veterans* and provides additional resources.

Connect to Canada's Veteran transition ecosystem

Canada has an abundance of resources and engaged actors ready to help support employers, Veterans, and their families. Visit the Canadian Armed Forces Transition Group's trusted National Resource Directory (NRD).

Find and attract Veteran jobseekers

Recruit Veterans using the Government of Canada Job Bank. Create an account to post a job.

Join the popular Hire a Veteran LinkedIn group.

Learn how to hire a Veteran through Veterans Affairs Canada (VAC).

Register with VAC as a Veteran Employer by sending an email or completing the registration form.

Find your local Canadian Armed Forces (CAF) Transition Centre. Contact your local centre for referrals, tips, and advice on connecting with Veteran jobseekers in your community.

Find out if you're eligible for the Compensation for Employers of Reservists Program.

If your Veteran employees need additional training, they may qualify for the Education and Training Benefit.

Check out the Canadian websites of large enterprises for inspiration and examples of how they promote their interest in hiring Veterans. Pay attention to how they advertise careers to Veterans.

Join the growing list of Veteran Ready Employers across Canada.

Explore all of Challenge Factory's work to close the gap between employers and Veterans: Hiring military Veterans.

- Infographic about shifts in employer perceptions of Veterans
- Infographic about the confidence levels that employers experience over six months after using a resource

Career management

Retain and Gain series of career management playbooks:

- Career management for small business
- Career management for non-profits and charities
- Career management for the public sector

Explore the glossary of military to civilian career transition terms to learn more.

Military-to-civilian translation

Browse military occupations to understand the diversity of skills, experience, and expertise that Veterans develop during their military careers.

MNET: Convert military occupations to their civilian equivalents or civilian occupations to their military equivalents.

Military to Civilian Employment: A Career Practitioner's Guide: A great resource for more information on translating military to civilian language.

Challenge Factory's Veteran hiring resources

Here's everything you need to know about Challenge Factory's three research-backed Veteran hiring resources.

The Canadian Guide to Hiring Veterans

Download your free digital copy or purchase a print copy.

Hidden Talent: A Challenge Factory Podcast

Listen wherever you get your podcasts.

MasterClass in Hiring: Tap into the Hidden Talent Pool of Canada's Veterans

Enroll for free to become a certified Veteran Ready Employer.

RESEARCH METHODOLOGY

Since 2012, Challenge Factory has been working to close the gap between employers and the hidden talent pool of Canada's military Veterans. Through our research, consulting, and training, we raise awareness about the benefits of hiring Veterans, give employers tools that will make hiring easier, and draw on Veterans' knowledge to make sure we get it right.

At the centre of our work is a research-to-practice service model. We conduct rigorous research so that the consulting, program development, and workforce solutions we provide to employers and other clients are grounded in evidence-based and data-driven insights and expertise.

The section details the research methodologies used to develop the first edition of *The Canadian Guide to Hiring Veterans* and measure the impact of Challenge Factory's Veteran hiring resources. It also details the program development and Veteran transition ecosystem mapping work that has informed the development of the second edition of the *Guide*.

Explore the full timeline of Challenge Factory's work with Veterans and employers across Canada.

Developing the first edition of *The Canadian Guide to Hiring Veterans*

To bring new insights to employers, hiring managers, and everyone interested in the participation of Veterans in Canada's civilian workforce, Challenge Factory used a multi-tiered methodology when conducting research as part of the development of the first edition of *The Canadian Guide to Hiring Veterans*.

Original data was collected through two sources. First, the managers of mature Veteran hiring programs at large enterprises were interviewed between November and December 2019. The semi-structured interviews explored their recruitment and employment practices, their opinions about Veterans in the workplace, and lessons they have learned over time and through experience. A loose interview schedule was used to guide the discussions.

Interview schedule:

- An introduction that describes Challenge Factory, the research project, and its goals

- Broad questions and topics of conversation meant to provoke thoughtful discussions, such as:

    1. How would you describe your Veteran hiring program? How long has it been established? What are its goals?

    2. What are your program's greatest successes?

    3. How do you go about promoting your Veteran hiring program and advertising jobs to Veterans?

    4. What advice about Veterans would you give to organizations with limited HR resources?

    5. If you were just beginning to hire Veterans, what would have made your job easier?

    6. Is there anything you would like to add?

- A conclusion that describes the type of follow-up that interviewees can expect from Challenge Factory in the future.

Second, more than 100 small- to medium-sized enterprises (SMEs) completed a psychometric survey between June 2019 and February 2020 about their perceptions of Veterans. Participation requests were delivered to more than 400 SMEs based in Ontario through association outreach and individual emails. Survey responses were screened out if participants worked for a company that has more than 500 employees or a mandate that concerns Veterans or military support (e.g., service providers, non-profit advocacy groups, etc.). Data analysis was conducted using 92 completed survey responses.

Developed by TTI Success Insights, the survey asked participants to adopt the viewpoint of a Veteran and answer a series of psychometric questions and statements based on how they thought a Veteran would respond. The survey measured how participants perceive the behaviours, driving forces, acumen indicators, and competencies of Veterans. Data was also gathered about participants' demographic and workforce factors. The full survey took approximately 15-30 minutes to complete.

The development of the first edition of the *Guide* also drew on existing literature about Veterans and Challenge Factory's previous research, including a 2017 psychometric survey of 200 employers, Veterans, and active CAF members, and organizational engagement since 2018 with more than 4,700 Canadians as part of a national dialogue about the Future of Work. Challenge Factory's expertise on career development, labour market information, human resources, and other aspects of the world of work (e.g., ageing populations, emerging technologies, other drivers of change) was also incorporated at every stage of the project.

The data was analyzed to identify key trends, gaps in and needs for knowledge about Veterans, and design principles for the project output. Once a working draft of the *Guide* was prepared, it was delivered to employers, Veterans, and active CAF members for beta testing. Feedback was solicited about the content and formatting of the *Guide*, its usability and usefulness, and any other ideas, questions, or concerns. The results of the testing were used to refine the first edition of the *Guide* for publication.

Conducting a national impact study of Veteran hiring resources

In 2021, Challenge Factory used our previous research and *The Canadian Guide to Hiring Veterans* to create two companion resources, MasterClass in Hiring: Tap into the Hidden Talent Pool of Canada's Veterans, and Hidden Talent: A Challenge Factory Podcast. In 2022, we conducted a national impact study to measure the impact that the three Veteran hiring resources have on employers—because understanding how resources help is as important as creating them.

Primary data collection consisted of four online survey questionnaires with business owners, organizational leaders, and hiring managers across Canada. The surveys were both cross-sectional and longitudinal, and designed to elicit data about respondents general hiring practices, use of the hiring resources, and perceptions of military Veterans.

This approach allowed us to conduct a combination of descriptive and analytical research. Descriptive research investigates the "what" of an unknown and focuses on describing, comparing, and measuring, while analytical research investigates the "how" and "why" of an unknown and focuses on understanding cause and effect.

We recruited study participants from the project team's professional networks, circulated the Call for Participants to professional associations across Canada, and sent out "cold call" emails using publicly accessible business directories.

Study participants chose one of the three hiring resources to explore, completed the first survey before beginning it (pre-intervention), then completed the second survey immediately after (post-intervention). This cross-sectional research allowed us to gather data about participants' self-reported use of the resources, as well as assess the resources' immediate impact on their knowledge, skills, and mindsets with respect to hiring and Veterans.

Study participants completed a third survey three months after initially exploring their hiring resource of choice, and a fourth survey six months after exploring it. This longitudinal research allowed us to track any self-reported longer-term changes in participants' behaviours, preferences, and attitudes about the hiring resources and Veterans.

In addition to these four survey questionnaires, we collected two sets of data from the MasterClass study participants using the built-in evaluation tools provided by the online learning platform that the hiring resource is hosted on. The two sets of data are:

1. "Module round-up" surveys at the end of each of the five learning modules

2. Progress reports about each user's activities and completion rate

Analyzing the data, we identified:

- key patterns and insights about employers' hiring practices, use of the resources, and perceptions of Veterans;

- gaps in and needs for employer knowledge, learning, or awareness raising about Veterans;

- curriculum design principles for employer-based hiring resources;

- future directions for Challenge Factory research; and,

- recommendations that can inform transition and job development programs offered to Veterans and employers through VAC, CAF, and other third parties.

Before publication of our analysis, drafts were circulated to the project's advisory committee for review and validation. Their feedback was used to refine, deepen, and finalize our analysis and insights.

Due to the heavy commitment required of participants and project time constraints, this study used a small sample size of 26 business owners, organizational leaders, and hiring managers. Participants came from SMEs and non-profit organizations across the country, including the Northwest Territories, Yukon, British Columbia, Alberta, Saskatchewan, Manitoba, Ontario, Quebec, New Brunswick, and Newfoundland and Labrador.

Program development and Veteran transition ecosystem mapping

In 2022, Challenge Factory created a new program for small business owners and Veterans called the Veterans and Small Business Community Challenge (VSBCC). This was a free experiential training program designed to accelerate the recruitment, onboarding, and hiring of Veterans by small businesses across Canada. Small business owners and Veterans took part in three training sessions each, earning a Veteran Ready Employer certificate or Small Business Acumen micro-credential.

This program fostered stronger community engagement between small businesses, SME-serving organizations, Veteran-serving organizations, and Veterans. We provided a forum that connected employers in need of labour with people who were looking for work.

In 2023-2024, Challenge Factory partnered with True Patriot Love on a multi-tiered project to advance our organizations' shared vision: A holistic, systems-focused approach to make Canadian provinces and territories more Veteran Friendly.

First, we mapped the Veteran transition ecosystem in Ontario and liaised with Veterans Affairs Canada and the Canadian Armed Forces (Transition Group) to integrate strategies and activities across all organizations. This included developing a dictionary of terms and program catalogue to summarize the various types of available programs and supports.

Second, we brought together more than ten large employers to collaborate and share Veteran hiring and retention best practices. Learnings from these employers informed the development of case studies and tools that could be used not only by large employers, but also by SMEs.

Third, for SMEs and Veterans, we developed the Veteran Friendly Ontario (VFO) Challenge, an experiential five-session training program designed to improve the hiring competence of small businesses and increase the employment prospects of Veterans.

The results of the national impact study, VSBCC program, and VFO project were used to develop the second edition of *The Canadian Guide to Hiring Veterans*.

NOTES AND REFERENCES

[1] TTI Success Insights. "Controlling Emotions in the Workplace: The Impact on Your Bottom Line." February 2011. https://s3-us-west-2.amazonaws.com/images.ttisi.com/wp-content/uploads/2016/04/18094825/wp_controlling_emotions_in_the_workplace.pdf.

[2] Fortange, André. "Benefitting from a Strong Employment Value Proposition." *CEB HR Consulting*, 2012.

[3] Siaroff, Emree. "Asking Better Questions: A Culture Blueprint that Works." *Workforce Architecture* (Spring/Summer 2022). https://community.challengefactory.ca/asking-better-questions-a-culture-blueprint-that-works/.

[4] CEB Corporate Leadership Counsel. "Introduction to EVP: CEB's Employment Value Proposition Framework." *CEB HR Consulting*, 2015.

[5] Sweet, Jill, Alain Poirier, Teresa Pound, and Linda VanTil. "Well-Being of Canadian Regular Force Veterans: Findings from LASS 2019 Survey." *Veterans Affairs Canada Research Directorate Technical Report*, October 2020, pp. 5. https://publications.gc.ca/collections/collection_2020/acc-vac/V3-1-7-2020-eng.pdf.

[6] Statistics Canada. "Canadian Survey on Disability, 2017 to 2022." *Government of Canada*, December 2023. https://www150.statcan.gc.ca/n1/daily-quotidien/231201/dq231201b-eng.htm.

[7] Sweet, Jill, Alain Poirier, Teresa Pound, and Linda VanTil. "Well-Being of Canadian Regular Force Veterans: Findings from LASS 2019 Survey." *Veterans Affairs Canada Research Directorate Technical Report*, October 2020, pp. 12. https://publications.gc.ca/collections/collection_2020/acc-vac/V3-1-7-2020-eng.pdf.

[8] Statistics Canada, "Table 98-10-0386-01, Highest Level of Education by Geography: Canada, Provinces, and Territories." *Government of Canada*. https://doi.org/10.25318/9810038601-eng.

[9] Sweet, Jill, Alain Poirier, Teresa Pound, and Linda VanTil. "Well-Being of Canadian Regular Force Veterans: Findings from LASS 2019 Survey." *Veterans Affairs Canada Research Directorate Technical Report*, October 2020, pp. 11. https://publications.gc.ca/collections/collection_2020/acc-vac/V3-1-7-2020-eng.pdf.

[10] Sweet, Jill, Alain Poirier, Teresa Pound, and Linda VanTil. "Well-Being of Canadian Regular Force Veterans: Findings from LASS 2019 Survey." *Veterans Affairs Canada Research Directorate Technical Report*, October 2020, pp. 12. https://publications.gc.ca/collections/collection_2020/acc-vac/V3-1-7-2020-eng.pdf.

[11] MacLean, Mary Beth, Linda VanTil, Jill Sweet, Alain Poirier, and Kris McKinnon. "Factors Associated with Work Satisfaction among Veterans." *Journal of Military, Veteran, and Family Health* (Vol. 4, No. 1), April 2018, p. 33–41. https://doi.org/10.3138/jmvfh.2017-0013.

www.ingramcontent.com/pod-product-compliance
Lightning Source LLC
Chambersburg PA
CBHW071504210326
41597CB00018B/2681